Rachel Eliza Griffiths

CARL PHILLIPS

Speak Low

Carl Phillips is the author of nine previous books of poems, including *Quiver of Arrows: Selected Poems, 1986–2006*; *Riding Westward*; and *The Rest of Love*, a National Book Award finalist. He teaches at Washington University in St. Louis.

T0057935

Also by Carl Phillips

POETRY

In the Blood

Cortège

From the Devotions

Pastoral

The Tether

Rock Harbor

The Rest of Love

Riding Westward

Quiver of Arrows: Selected Poems, 1986–2006

PROSE

Coin of the Realm: Essays on the Life and Art of Poetry

TRANSLATION

Sophocles: Philoctetes

Speak Low

Speak Low

CARL PHILLIPS

Farrar, Straus and Giroux

NEW YORK

Farrar, Straus and Giroux
18 West 18th Street, New York 10011

Printed in the United States of America
Published in 2009 by Farrar, Straus and Giroux
First paperback edition, 2010

The Library of Congress has cataloged the hardcover edition as follows:
Phillips, Carl, 1959–
     Speak low / Carl Phillips.— 1st ed.
     p.   cm.
     ISBN: 978-0-374-26716-2 (alk. paper)
     I. Title.

PS3566.H476 S64 2009
811'.54—dc22

                                        2008046000

Paperback ISBN: 978-0-374-53216-1

Designed by Jonathan D. Lippincott

www.fsgbooks.com

P1

. . . and I could feel my self carried with a mighty Force and Swiftness towards the shore a very great Way . . .
                                                            —Daniel Defoe

Contents

Speak Low 3

Southern Cross 4

Mirror, Window, Mirror 6

Conquest 7

Rubicon 8

*

Captivity 11

Lighting the Lamps 13

To Drown in Honey 14

Gold on Parchment 15

In a Perfect World 17

Detachment 18

The River in Motion and in Stillness 20

Happiness 21

Distortion 22

Porcelain 24

The Damned 25

Directions from Here 26

Night Song 27

Storm 28

Topaz 30

The Moonflowers 31
Late Empire 32
Volition 34
Reciprocity 36
Now in Our Most Ordinary Voices 37
Naming the Stars 38
Beautiful Dreamer 40
The Plains of Troy 41
The Centaur 42
A Little Moonlight 44
Landfall 47
Living Together 48
Cloud Country 49
Fair Is Whatever the Gods Call Fair 53
The Raft 54

*

Sterling 57
Husk 58
Until There's Nothing, Just the Sea, a Sea of Leaves 60

*

Notes 65
Acknowledgments 67

Speak Low

Speak Low

The wind stirred—the water beneath it stirred accordingly . . .
The wind's pattern was its own, and the water's also. The
water in that sense was the wind's reflection. The wind was,
to the water, what the water was to the light that fell there,
or appeared to fall, spilling as if the light were a liquid, or as
if the light and the water it spilled across

                                            were now the same.
It is true that the light, like the water, assumed the pattern of
what acted upon it. But the water assumed also the shape
of what contained it, while the light did not. The light seemed
fugitive, a restiveness, the less-than-clear distance between
everything we know we should do, and all the rest—all
the rest that we do. Stirring, as the wind stirred it, the water
was water—was a form of clarity itself, a window we've
no sooner looked through than we've abandoned it for what
lies past that: a view, and then what comes

                                            into view, or might,
if we watch patiently enough, steadily—so we believe, wishing
for what, by now, even we can't put a name to, but feel certain
we'll recognize, having done so before. It looked, didn't it,
just like harmlessness. A small wind. Some light on water.

Southern Cross

When I woke, I was still on top of him. Darkness, to
darkness. The taking of leave again until leave-taking
becomes, itself, souvenir, the only one I keep—that's
worth keeping. See how it begins to look like courtesy,
in the right light,

                with a little distance? Steadily, without
filling it, not ever, a silence falls into, through, into that
narrow space between what I'd rather not know and
everything I know. It falls like chance, what's possible,
and the possibilities fall open in turn to every side of me,
a first falling crop of snow, doors that the wrong wind
sometimes gets sudden hold of,

                      then loses, as now.
When it comes to the gods always crippling those whom
they love most, as a way of ensuring in the beloved both
fear and need—where, in fact, does it ever say so? Did I
make that up, too? All of it? It's a myth in my head? And
if I've been living as if it weren't a myth, but something
more than that—a truth, instructive?

*

I think the sea must be,
to the ocean, as disappointment is to sorrow, that it's like
the difference between granting mercy to none of those
who suffer, and withholding it from all who do: how they're
not the same things, exactly; I don't care

how it seems.
When I woke, I was still on top of him—still inside him.

The sea isn't far from us, it can't be, I remember thinking:
through the dark, I could smell the sea. It isn't ocean, at all.

Mirror, Window, Mirror

Yes, any sky at night, when the flickering of snow-lightning gently
punctuates it, whatever it is when it's
not bewilderment, or daring, and
not fear either, also
the mottled bark of sycamores
in autumn for where the skin
was like that. Yes.

*

—But more like arousal,

or more instead like the mind just
before the idea of arousal courses
bluntly through it?

*

         That part about the body
asking for it,

to be broken into—is that the first, or last part?

Conquest

Speaking to himself, I think, not me, *You have wanted*
more than was yours to wish for, he said—as if even
to wishing the laws of modesty and excess could be applied,
and should be. We slept. I dreamed.

We'd sworn
never to do harm; then sworn instead to keep trying hard
not to— A kind
                    of progress . . .

                              *

                    In the dream, he was powerful:
a hawk,
            or hawklike—this time, easily distinguishable
from the gentler animals and that relentlessness with which,
like beaten slaves by now
                    used to it, they rise, and they fall.

Rubicon

Like that feeling inside the mouth as it makes of obscenity
a new endearment. Like a rumormonger without sign among
the deaf,
        the speechless. Having been able, once, not only
to pick out the one crow in a cast of ravens, but to parse darker,
even more difficult distinctions: weakness and martyrdom;
waves, and the receding fact of them as they again
                                come back;
bewilderment and, as if inescapable, that streak of cruelty to
which by daybreak we confess ourselves resigned, by noon
accustomed, by night
              devoted—feverish: *now a tinderbox
in flames, now the flames themselves*, that moment in intimacy
when sorrow, fear, and anger cross in unison the same face,
what at first can seem almost
                      a form of pleasure, a mistake as
easy, presumably, as it's forgivable. I suspect forgetting will be
a very different thing: more rough, less blue, more lit, and patternless.

Captivity

I

In the book of the body that is yours—where it's never as late
as I had thought it was, though I routinely fail, forget still
not to call it my own—

                  in the book of my body that is finally
yours only, the wind picks up, the clouds of everything that
I've been wrong about in this life pass singly overhead as if
for review, their cast
                  shadows meanwhile, with the unstable
camaraderie of exiles from the start united solely in their desire,
for now, to be anywhere else, little more than that,
                                    pass also . . .

Oh, sometimes it is as if desire itself had been given form, and
acreage, and I'd been left for lost there. Amazement grips me,

I grip it back, the book shuts slowly: Who shuts it? You?

II

Memory, awareness. Expectation. A light rain falls . . . That
there are three of us in the room
                                    isn't clear at first, though it is
always the three of us, naked, strangers who nevertheless belong
together, but so briefly, I've no sooner assigned names to what
happens here, the names detach, reassign themselves: this one,
and now this one . . .

                              It makes little difference, any more than
vision does, in a room this dark. It's not by vision I tell apart
the two of them, but how the one smells like something checked
coming gradually unchecked, neither rage exactly, nor triumph

mixed with it, but not unlike that; to the other a touch that brings
everything back: the promises in their not-yet-broken state,
the brokenness after; the distilled sorrow, inside that—

                                       *

—How delicately, as if with care, the dark holds the nakedness that
is the three of us, turning each to each, unappeasable, in constellation . . .

Lighting the Lamps

I've bloomed twice in this life already.
Once, as a fever, in its blooming.

The second time—

         It was like when a raven unfolds
its blackery to its fullest span and, having risen,
glides now at that angle which suggests the glamour
of a thing stolen for a last chance—brief,
maybe, but at least resonant—at a life
that's better. Doesn't pattern require—to be seen
as pattern—not just repetition but, as well, eventually,
the interruption of it? As the shore
is the wave's interruption? As mistake interrupts
what had shown no flaw? What I know
is the raven was never sorrow. Wasn't—voiced,
or silent—the sign for it. It crossed the meadow. It
pulled its raven-shadow with it. It disappeared.

To Drown in Honey

Now the leaves rush, greening, back. Back now,
the leaves push greenward. —Some such song, or
close to. I forget the most of it. His voice, and
the words pooling inside it. And the light for once
not sexual, just light. The light, as it should be . . .

You can build for yourself a tower to signal from.
Can become a still life. A slow ruin. You can
walk away. They all say that. Sir, I see no way

out of it. I have put my spade to the black loam
that the mind at one moment lets pass for truth,
at the next, oblivion. I have considered. I know
what's buried there: emptiness and renunciation and
ash, and ash . . . Why, then, so suddenly—overnight
almost—all the leaves again? Why now, rushing back?

Gold on Parchment

The rocks here are volcanic. They rise from the sea—
stand above it—only to be covered by it, and then
disclosed again in the wave's receding. The waves
sheathe the rock's face with departure's pattern—
then the pattern goes too . . . Earlier, when the tide
was low, you could have seen a lone egret walking
the zones between the rocks: entirely white; hunting;
what was it hunting? Where were you? The waves
broke farther from shore, so what passed now between
the rocks was all sea foam, its white the same white
as the egret's, against it the bird seeming, a moment,
to have disappeared, invisibility seemed a thing worth
envying, though I do not forget, mostly, the difference
between the kind of invisibility one can wield—a form
of power—and the other kind, that gets imposed from
outside, and later fastens like character, or dye, as if
invisibility were instead a dye, and the self a spill
of linen, Egyptian cotton: *whore*—

                                        Wave covers rock,
and then draws back, recessional. The rock glistens
with it. Pretty, isn't it? —Isn't it? In the day, it's like
a boy's hand passing somewhere between leisurely
and impatiently back through his hair again, until it

lies in the place that—today, at least—he thinks he'd
like it to forever. Your hand still does that . . . But in
the night—even a moonless night—the wave passes
not like a hand at all, but like recognition, as when
the mind at last recognizes the body's corruption as
absolute and (unlike a wave) irreversible, and the body—
or the mind's idea of it—re-emerges, stripped of its
former willfulness, perhaps, but not of its will to be
free, more free, and not of its indifference to the costs
of freedom. *Memory as a space, like any other, to be
crossed or not crossed, regretless, any time we choose*—
I remember that. We called ourselves the lucky ones.
Called the sea—the sea: we could turn our backs to it.

In a Perfect World

Equally, the black lake that the skiff sails across,
and the skiff also. Wingbeat. A belief in evil
having not yet displaced entirely a belief in the power
to turn evil away. Laughter. Any number of small
voices in a field unfolding. Patterns like the one
where arrogance leads to shame, shame to anger,
until from anger—via the suffering called loss, called

grieving for it: at last, compassion. Hoofbeat. Bluegrass.
Persuasion slowly brushstroking its way back into
what had seemed the world. A shadow prowling
the not-so-clear-anymore perimeter of *Who says so?*
A single mother-of-pearl stud catching parts of the light—
for now, holding them. Troy is burning. Let us
make of what's left a sturdiness we can use to the end.

Detachment

It was lonely, though we did not say so. Height
of summer, the usual crew

of questions, sporting
themselves as if each were a muscle, and flawless:
what is memory? what is time? what will deliverance,
versus what we wished for, turn out to have been
really? —Questions that, if they did require us
or, for that matter, any answer, had a strange way
of showing it, seeming to stall on the air before
drifting across it, lazily, like blood with a drawl to it,
then vanishing,

whatever it was that we'd been
afraid of, so afraid, drifting with it, past the garden's
bright progress,

whatever was left, meanwhile, of
the old forbearance that, in small, then in not so
small stages, we'd said no to—not because it was
any less desirable than it had ever been, but because
in its presence we felt defeated where we'd grown

so used to feeling otherwise—that vanished also,
into the garden's cooler, more lightless parts, where
the ferns began, their fronds rising severally before

leaning away, each from the other, but gently, as
when to turn away in the night, after, from another's
body doesn't have to mean something less—or
more, either—just a different closeness,

                                the leaves
of the fronds dividing, redividing, not so much like
knowledge as curiosity, what knowing comes from,

not the wound, but the mind's insistence that we put
our hands to it and, having touched it, push deeper
still,

      where lies remembering, the pain reminding us,
the hands stopped now, how if it was sexual at all,
any of it, if they came—since on their faces lay
no sign—it could mostly be told only by listening
carefully as, as if half-reluctant, the hand

                                  draws back—

The River in Motion and in Stillness

As if with the satisfaction of a near-impossible task
brought finally, and with no little struggling, to absolute
accomplishment, he lifts his ruined face up from beside

the other's face, just as ruined, despite the sun being at that
angle that makes what ordinarily gets taken for flaw
very briefly what it also is: a loveliness, and something

strange, original . . . Hour when the particular blunder of
misjudgment, winging its way more forcibly toward us,
can become almost a kind of truth that, though no longer

believed in, still seems worth longing for. Some of us
surrender the self. Some withhold it. You can see how
the river, ever so slightly, turns here, just before descending.

Happiness

The tears of Achilles were nothing compared
to the ones his horses famously wept at the death
of Patroclus, whom Achilles had loved. Immortal,
and yet earthbound, hovering around their disbelief,
around their instinct not to believe—as a bee will hover,

fooled at first, over freshly spilled semen—they wept,
I think, not for the fact of death, not out of their inability
to make, *from* fact, some understanding, but because
they wept. They were, in this way at least, strangely
human. Then they were horses again, doomless,

who could not know or say what weeping was.

Distortion

Having opened to their fullest, they opened further—
Now the peonies, near to breaking, splay groundward,
some even touch the ground, and though I do understand,
yes, that they're not the not-so-lovely-after-all example
of how excess, even in its smallest forms, seems to have
its cost, I think it anyway,

                I even think they look, more
than a little bit, like rough sex once it's gone where, of
course, it had to—do you know what I mean, his smell
on you after, like those parts of the gutted deer that
the men bring home with them, fresh from the hunt,
as if you were like that now, the parts, not the smell, I
mean as if you were his, all you'd ever wanted to be,
and how you almost believe that?

                    Do you see that too?

According to Augustine, it's a distortion of the will
that leads to passion, a slavish obedience to passion that
leads to habit, until habit in turn becomes hunger, a need.
—What is it about logic, when delivered unflinchingly,
that makes a thought like that sound true, whether true

or not? Significant of nothing but a wind that, rising
suddenly, falls as suddenly again back, the trees swing
briefly in the same direction, as if I couldn't quite
admit, yet, to a kind of grace

                              in synchronicity, and had
asked for proof, and the trees were one part of it, another
the light at this late-afternoon hour when it works both
against and in the body's favor, like camouflage—which
in the end is only distortion by a prettier name. I know
all about that. You can call it heartlessness, an indifference
to ruin, a willed inability to be surprised by it—you'd be
mistaken. Don't go. Let me show you what it looks like
when surrender, and an instinct not to, run side by side.

Porcelain

As when a long forgetfulness lifts suddenly, and what
we'd forgotten—as we look at it squarely, then again
refuse to look—is our own
                              inconsequence, yes, it was
mostly like that, sex as both an act of defacement and—
as if the two were the same thing—votive offering,
insofar as the leaves
                        also were a kind of offering, or could
at least be said to be, as they kept on falling the way leaves
do: volitionless, from different heights, and in the one direction.

The Damned

With an ease considerably past what even we'd expected,
the brush took fire. The birds unhid themselves, flew
abruptly elsewhere, like shame when, from the wrong end
of a foundering argument, it at last lets go. Is it risk, for
example, if what gets lost goes unregretted? Or if there
is any risk, then where, except awhile in the head?

Shipwreck in a sunset that makes everything look wrecked,
and lovely; the shot deer that keeps running, uselessly, October
and death breaking in front of and closing shut behind her.
Fullness. Emptiness. Violence. Calm. *Turn it off, turn it
off,* a voice was shouting: And the fire burning, like fire.

Directions from Here

The figs at Jane's.
             Migrants harvesting the Cabernet—
the brown of their hands— The blue in twilight . . .
The talismanic becoming merely notational. You
as Oblivion riding bareback on Notoriety, my
favorite horse. You the boy who, in sleep, briefly

touches himself, then leaves his hand there, for
no reason except warmth, that reassurance that,
in the dark, the body gives more reliably than
the saints or prayer can. A silence, as of snow,
for miles. That moment in grandeur when
the one thing left sustaining it—a belief in grandeur—

itself collapses. A kind of gift, we thought.
Masochism. Fever dream. The way we kept falling
each time half-longingly. Enough. Now speak
of ruin—that appetite for it, by which the one
who loves knows
             most immediately his beloved.

Night Song

Servitude. Conquest. The one who, from the hip, keeps
pushing himself up into the other's mouth. The one who
takes from behind. The more prismatic of the Roman
emperors—at each turn of the light, yet another shade

of a near-unstoppable will-to-power, of humiliation's
not-so-strange allure. Later, those emperors of the almost-
finished second century, who by their own example make
a case for submission to what resists control: Hadrian

falls for the boy Antinous; Marcus Aurelius for a stoicism
in the face of corruption, plague, barbarians . . . Conquest
and servitude; suffering, and suffering's famous ability
to bring about a patience that pleasure ultimately has little

time for. I close my eyes. I remain persuadable. I give
up what I can. Who's to say what will not be useful?

Storm

From the waist down, at least,
nothing unfamiliar. Cypress trees. The catalpa,
its seedpods hanging like shadow-icicles. And the light
around them. And the bodies that

                        enter the light, and leave it,
your own among them, but as when the body seems
most to want, impossibly, to step free of itself, oblivion
of wish,

         of wishing. —About sanctuary, how over
time it makes the birds come closer: how that's different
from trust—isn't it? *What the fuck do you think you're
looking at*, he says softly. What a thing

                  to say—
The mind protecting itself by shutting down an intimacy
that, most likely, won't be returned. Why expect it? As if
that were the mind's chief purpose, to resist a fall, though
falling's what the body

                  does best. Is quick to rise for. Moving
toward you with all the ceremony of many wings at
once outspread, a holiday, descending. The dark adjusts
itself, settles its wings inside you. The shadows that
strut the dark

          open and fold like hope, a paper fan, violence

in its pitch and fall, like waves—above them, the usual
seabirds, their presumable

                             indifference to chance, its
blond convergences . . . As when telling cruelty apart
from chivalry can come to seem irrelevant, or not anymore
the main point. He touches himself here,

                                   and here. Directive.
Turns his face away. It can look like ransom. Now it looks
like privilege, now recklessness, now triumph, gravel-and-blood,
humiliation, lovely, now strict refrain, he taketh my hand
in his.

Topaz

Meanwhile, belief
elsewhere enough abounding. Ritual's
not what I mean, though—

                  or not exactly. Not the bones
of ceremony, either: insufficient, finally, to our longing
now to fill a space, and now—getting filled—to be the space
itself . . . But as when the body lies restless, votive, in a nakedness
with which holiness has at once everything and very little
to do.

    What does it
matter that, for the ghost majority, the god Apollo likely never
existed, slaughtered no one, strung nobody's body up from
some wild and

              half-broken-looking olive tree, the flayed limbs
going steadily more vintage in what there was, still, of any light
at all,

    if you know better than that, if I'm everything
you wished for?

The Moonflowers

It's as if the dark, which had before
just been context, gave to vulnerability
a permission, almost: fleshy saucers of
spilled cream, so many parchment fists,
unfisting; and now, in pieces, the delicate
mask of an indifference offered radically
up against what, each time, seems as
unthinkable, as unexpected, as when,

in the long dream of retraction, that sea
that is finally not a sea, but what else
to call it, begins again its shifting, and
though to every push of the will forward
there's something noble—which is to say,
something lonely, also—it's too late.

Late Empire

I mean after the lashing.
After the welts that the lash gave rise to have
healed so beautifully, we forget where they were. *Here*,
we say, pointing vaguely, as toward a bird that
could as easily be a sparrow hawk,

any other falcon—as if it made no real difference now,
though it must, somewhere. It should. As between
grand events and those that are less grand; or as when
the Greeks described fate as a thing of substance, weighable
on a set of scales, pourable into steep urns—one for happiness,

another for woe—and the urns tipped accordingly by Zeus
as, from the vantage point that only a god can have,
he saw fit—which is only a way of
understanding fate, not a form of acceptance,
not a road to get there . . . There's a kind of fragility

that confounds appearances, where what little strength
that the body has left to it, though almost none at all, seems
inexhaustible. And there's a fragility that is most like
what sex amounts to when stripped of justice
and imagination: one more way of leaning up against

and at the same time containing the fact
of death, even as we ignore it or, for a time,
lose track, wondering instead at the heave-and-shallow
that the wind can be, sometimes, as if the wind
were a sea of water, the world presenting itself in

the smallest of shards that, very briefly,
surface—then they fall back away. Words like *torture*,
and *worshipful*. *Winnow* and *chaff*. Fairness
continuing to have nothing to do with it. No one gets to decide.
Just look at all the damage I might never have done.

Volition

We lay steep in summertime.
We'd let our bodies by their own gravity settle into
the stillness of it, where they moved now with the sluggish
grace of plants under water, when they moved at all. Peaceful,
but the kind of peace that comes just after the laying of
arms down in surrender, which is to say, it felt a lot like defeat,
as if we'd come to an end, finally, not so much of wickedness itself
as of an impulse toward it that we'd long ago, having straddled it,
thought we'd mastered—and yet here we were, as if thrown,

dismounted, but never quite hitting the hard ground
of reason, reason itself having given way, we had nothing but
instinct now, in a world where moral valence no longer seemed
to apply: a bruise could be triumph could be one more
sunset could be perversion, and the question was not
How to tell the difference but *Who's to say we have to,*
or should? It was as if morality, like light, were now refractable:
we could see the colors, but what do colors mean, ever, except

what we want them to, and nothing at all? We lay steep
in a stillness that anyone might confuse with paralysis, or
with a stalemate between recklessness and detachment, as they
vie for possession of a single body—but it wasn't that:

couldn't we turn away whenever we chose to? *Any moment,*
we kept telling ourselves—so often, that it seemed sometimes we
already had turned, but as from a violent hand to which, nevertheless,
the mind still attaches some small affection: we draw the hand
briefly close again, so as almost to kiss it, yes, before letting it go.

Reciprocity

Rest now. All that ruggedness, blood-pain, and blindness-to-its-
own-illusions that, classically, the establishing of new frontiers
has always required—the work
                              of empire: that was then.

In its wake, the fallen leaves rise and fall again, like the feet of
gods long ago deposed, shambling
                              nevertheless into their dusty,
once-fine arena. The gods look gently out on the staggered crowd.
And—very gently—the crowd, applauding, surprises even itself.

Now in Our Most Ordinary Voices

There's a kind of shadowland that one body makes, entering
another; and there's a shadowland the body contains always
within itself, without resolution—as mystery a little more
often, perhaps, should be . . . For a moment, somewhere
between the two, I can see myself as I begin to think
you must see me: a stranger to helplessness,
spouting things like *To know is to live flayed* and *Ambition
means turning the flesh repeatedly back—toward the whip,
not away*, I can still hear myself saying that, believing it—
now it all sounds wrong . . .

                  Look at the trees: willows, mostly—
They move in that way willows move—as if wanting to
pace themselves, slow, impossibly, in a building wind, as if
the wind were fate, and the trees' response one that could
maybe make a difference. Frankly, it's the inevitability part
that I most adore, still, in the inevitable. It makes of blame
an irrelevance. We'll take up once more the two positions that—
favoring depth over range—we've mastered, finally: this time it's
your turn to be the bonfire; I'll be the distance through which
the bonfire, unspecifiable, could at first be any small point
of restlessness—lit, contained—in a blackening field.

Naming the Stars

By perspective, I meant how

                eventually every landscape wouldn't
have to include defilement, or any other outrage, getting smaller
each time we looked back on it,

                or forgot not to. An armload of
millet and sunflowers could, despite the fact of July, just like that,
turn the room October. I believed suffering happened

                not because
it had to, but because it happened. Was all of that, too, a dream?

                *

It's a question that's asked early in Homer's *Iliad*; Helen asks it,
questioning everything she's known, or thought she did, before.
No one answers her because, as is consistently the case in Homer,
part of the point is

                it's all inevitable, even the silences. Back
then, of course—much more than now—there were many silences,
in which to appreciate all the more

                completely what, elsewhere,
Homer also means: the disproportion, for example, between how
the hero conducts his life and how

                unremarkably like everyone
else he at last must leave it; or a certain stateliness, if not always

to death in its every form, then to its strange, unmistakable cadence,
at once seasonal and—and
                        all the time: now a field sparrow; now
a shadow in the field of my sparrowed hand . . .

                        *

                                    I remember less
what his name was, or what at least he called himself, than a habit
he had of laying the stronger of his two strong hands, after, across
my eyes,
            as if would close them,
                                as if suddenly ashamed for his
own nakedness, its
                    ungainly dismounting. *Why be ashamed,*
I'd forget to ask, each time, so that it seems now I must not have
cared—not badly; not badly enough . . .
                                    There's a moment when
the hero, having taken his helmet off, puts it on again, his muddied
and gut-spattered face looks somehow lovelier for the bronze
that frames it,
                it's almost forgivable, even the gods in their abrupt

desertion, everything they stood for— Let the conquering begin.

Beautiful Dreamer

And when the punishment becomes, itself, a pleasure?
When there's no night that goes unpunished? The larger
veins show like map work, as in *Here winds a river,*
here a road in summer, the heat staggering up from it
the way always, at triumph's outermost, less chromatic
edges, some sorrow staggers. Parts where the mud,
though the rains are history now, refuses still to
heal over. Parts

                untranslatable. Parts where, for whole
stretches, vegetation sort of strangling sort of makeshift
sheltering the forest floor. To the face, at the mouth
especially, that mix of skepticism, joy, and panic reminiscent
of slaves set free too suddenly. Too soon. —Which way's
the right way? New hunger by new hunger? Spitting
on weakness? Raising a fist to it? The falling mouth falls
farther. Opens. It says: *I was the Blue King. I led the dance.*

The Plains of Troy

It is Odysseus who, having seen his rival Ajax brought down
by madness, equates a life on earth with nothing—all of it
illusion. The Greek camp lies rippling in front of him
with the latest slaughter, with a seeming addiction to rank,
stamina, the cleanest distance from shame possible, and
to a longing that at once is sexual and somewhere also
has to do with war as the context without which
                                            value's shape
becomes barely discernible. Three horses turn softly,
simultaneous, in the wind's direction. A series of veils—
raised, and unraised: Is this what it comes to, the examined life?
Must it? The drive toward meaning not, in fact, in the face of
meaninglessness, but of irrelevance—to have meant,
without mattering finally—that more palpable darkness,
magisterially unfurling its wings, then folding them equally around
the sleepers, the awake and restless, the freshly raped, the slain?

The Centaur

And when there was nothing that lay between us,
not even the nothingness that had
come to mean something—had meant something
to me—
  we felt clumsy; irredeemable, somehow.
And reason, that had once had over lust an effect
like rinsing,
    now canceled it out. He wept openly,
like a man, like one who can't understand, or
won't accept it, that the decision
      to refrain from killing—
to cripple instead—is a human choice, finally,
not animal,
   the heart not so much broken as
left beating in a metaphysical kind of disrepair that gets
called a brokenness. When
     had the world become so
inexact, or ourselves, who had lived too long, perhaps,
inside it, so forgiving
    of inexactness?
He shook in the light. Beside me. His arms lay thrown
across my chest like a stole of foxheads, its glamour
stranded now, somewhere

                    between fetish and perverse
sorrow. It was as difficult to know, anymore,
the difference between being truly dissatisfied
and merely unastonished
                        as it was to look at him.
But I did look: small birds—a-sway, then
back again, as the bamboo sways them . . .
                                    I looked again:
a hatch of flies,
                in a false spring whose falseness
changes nothing of how it must feel, to have risen
up into the air for the first time.

A Little Moonlight

I

Given inconstancy, the resistless
affair that has been my body (as if
there were no place to go from anywhere except
deeper, into those spaces the hand makes by
tugging the flesh, where it is partable,
more open, or as if I believed, utterly, what
legend says about violation—how it leads
to prophecy, the god enters the body, the mouth
cracks open, and a mad fluttering, which
is the future, fills the cave, which is
desire, *luck and hazard, hazard and luck*),

I should perhaps regret more. But it's grown
so late: see how dark, outside?

II

Suspecting, even then,
that the best way to avoid being
broken by flaw would be to shape my life
around it—flaw coming slowly
to define the self, as shells make of the glass
that holds them a little kingdom
of sea—I followed him, and have only once
looked back. Oh, I contain him

as the lion's chest contains the arrow
that death displaces, effect always mattering
more than cause: pull the arrow free—
brandish it. By now it must weigh
almost nothing . . .

III

I agree, to hope for a thing is to believe in it,
or at least to want to. When does belief
become expectation? Like committing
a crime, confessing to it, and thinking
confession might equal apology, mistaking
apology for to wipe clean away,
you turn your face to me. —What?

Trees in a wind. Their mixed
invitation of leaves flourishing as if unstoppable,
as if foliage were the greater part of it, the part
I could love best, or should learn to say I do
more often. Tell me why, when what I loved
from the start was how eventually each leaf must go.

Landfall

From here, I can see that ritual is but a form of
routine charged with mystery, and the mystery is faith—
whatever, by now, that might be. Twilight. The usual
eyeful of stars appearing, looking the way stars at first
always do: locked; stable.

                    My friend, to whom
sadness had once felt almost too familiar—*Step into it*,
he used to say, *stare up and out from it*—tells me now
he misses it. He wants to know does that mean
he's happy?

                    In the dark, he turns to me. The silences
rise to either side of us: silence of intimacy when
estranged from risk; of risk itself when there's no one
to take it—nobody willing to; silence, by which the dead
can be told more easily apart from the merely broken . . .

Living Together

Love, death, ambition . . . Step back a little, and the fog
returns to what it always was—its own opinion,
not the right or wrong one. A finch settles
on a tiger lily like an intended kindness beneath
which the stem bends slightly, not so much
receiving as accommodating the new weight,

the way truth accommodates distortion, and can
still seem true. *What world? Whose wildering*
throne from which to watch it? Love? Death?
Ambition? I keep thinking about force—its
dehumanizing effect, both on the victim
and on the one who wields it. When the white moths

leave the white blow flowers that all but erase them
for a backdrop against which they're exposed
entirely, whether this is instinct, or a choice—and,
if a choice, one that rises from perversion, mistake,
blindness in its countless forms— Just this once,
pretend none of it matters: love; death; or ambition.

Cloud Country

As from a sea—
            as endless as we choose to believe it to be,
at rest, and in restlessness, its waves cresting, breaking,
now the latest idea about moral freedom, now a memory
of it, that dims until no longer trustworthy, the stuff
of legend—
            to wake each morning feels not like waking
but like having been washed up from dreamlessness onto

a shore of our own hard making that, gradually, we've
learned to stop trying
                        not to mistake for the natural world:
cricket-song giving to a field at night its fourth dimension,
or is that a recording or, even more persuasive, not
crickets at all but
                        something entirely machine-generated,
downloaded, virtual? With all the physics of an inflexible
law and, like catastrophe, hypnotic, it can seem as if this
has from the start been the inevitable tendency: first

a blurring of all but the most crude distinctions, and then
to the blurring
                        —a stone, indifference. Love and cruelty,

humility and the affectation of it, benevolence and *How's*
about I let you suck me off real slow. Who we were,
in a lineup beside four versions of what we've turned into,
and ourselves the victim, exhausted, confused, unable to
say with any real certainty

                      who did it, sure of nothing now
except what violation—if even that's correct—feels like
or, more exactly, all the things it isn't: not vengeance,
proof of nothing, nobody's clear point of reference,
not mutability, nor the blow-smitten thrall to it, nor
the master of it, coming back

                    for more . . . Ah, the lies
one sings to oneself against regretting,

                        which we no more
believe in than we do in forgiveness: not "Forgive and
forget"—no, our motto is "No forgiveness before
oblivion," after which, what can it mean to forgive, when

there's nothing there? It's not regret that we feel, but
a soft disdain for our own inability to call the kingdom
we've made out of fear, risk, outrage, and a schooled
detachment the narrow prison

                    it so clearly is. There's life

as we know it. And there is death—lots of it. In between,
though, to the air at times a sense
                              of possibility, its effect
delusional, so that often we
                        cannot help it, this feeling
inside us so close to an almost
                              uncontainable joy—
Moments when we're as blameless as we're invincible:
nowhere a hunger to be undone by, to have suffered
defeat beside . . . Just
                        the jackdaws in all their ragged black
shinery—part *Watch me*, part *Close your eyes*—and
everywhere the summer roses that, after years of having tried
to train them, we've let run rampant, until their wildness
is what we've come to love most
                              about them, especially
now, each rose completely blown open, for—already—it's

summer again, that most delicate part of it, when the energy
required to keep a life from faltering
                              starts—at first, barely
noticed—to outweigh the desire to, and now slowly descends.
Have we really gone past the point of saving ourselves, of

sparing others? And though the chance to take even our smaller
brutalities back keeps feeling far, and then farther away—
is it? The roses lie sprawled in stillness, as if broken at
last by their
                 own inadequacy. They lie as still as resistance.
One by one, we say aloud the names that, so long ago, we
took the time—we cared that much—to give to them. Such a
stupid tenderness. *Superstition, Gash, Blue Vestige, Wash Away.*

Fair Is Whatever the Gods Call Fair

He said: *You keep speaking like a man who knows*
exactly how he became what—what he's become, but
you don't; you don't know. Then he turned away.
The shore. The sky. The sea. Certain animal cries
that I called distinctive, once—like silver rings of
an almost too-delicate thinness,

                              tapping porcelain,
sometimes glass . . . World that's everything I've wanted
in this life—not so much the train, as the sound of
train-rumble rising through a stillness late in summer,
then fading, even as

                     the questions do: Is fate a gift
received, do we ourselves determine it, does it exist at all?
He says: *You must let the body fall sway to what at last*
it will, learn to look entirely, and

                          without trembling.
He stands in front of me. He undresses as if to do so
had the force of ritual—a stiff unwinding of what can't
be salvaged

                from around what can—until there's
nothing but the tangle of thorns he brandishes at each
wrist; at the ankles, pearls. —I'd forgotten pearls. The way
they give back a light unequal to the light that's cast on them.

The Raft

Color of rust, russet. Color of fall. I can lay my head
on the wet sand that is nobody's chest now—not a chest,
at all—or I can lift it. Why not lift it? More fugitive than
lost, more spent than stranded, if I've been no stranger
to disillusionment,

                    nor am I enslaved to it. *The one who*
wanted me just to hold him gently, the one whose mouth
was his only tenderness, the one with whom, about whom—
who was a light, as off of water, that kept unsettling like
thought itself, like the scrim of thinking when pierced
suddenly by what nothing but instinct, pure gut, explains—

Inside me, the old desires half-negotiate, half-meander
their way back again, find those places they never stray
too far from, or not for long. I had thought the truth
would be a falcon—for how it rarely soars, as much as for
that precision with which, on wings instead built for speed
mainly, it descends, then strikes. But it is not a falcon.
The truth is a raft, a rough-at-each-of-its-edges affair of many
sturdinesses lashed together. Standard beauty; realized
expectation. The lucky ones get to choose, and they choose
when they want to. From this distance, it's hard to tell at first.
The raft's moving closer, I think. Though it's still far away.

Sterling

Soon, we'll wake. We'll see
what's real. Soon, the woodcock startling suddenly up again, as much
out of hunger as from fear. I'll tell you
everything—whose clouds these are; who says so . . .

I lie under the stars the way people used to do. What was meant
by enough. In blood.
In cinders also.
Now the weather passes like truth,

and the truth like weather: from merely elusive to, at last,
resistant. Lopsided, battered, but still serviceable—what *is* memory?
A shield?
A shelter?

*

The stableboy leading the horse gently out to the reckless horseman.

Restless, the toss of hawthorn-shadow across the horse's brow.

Husk

Now the rain pools, in shallows.

Now the animals come, thirsting, closer.

Now a wordlessness prevailing the way
a wind prevails—
what could shift
anytime . . .

*

Sometimes the colony collapses.
The bees
don't come back, though not because of—as once
was thought—any
moral weakness, the idea of which continues

strangely to matter, even as, more and more,
it resists mattering.

*

Fallibility,

plash—

and here, where the longer
branches jut out over the water, the leaves'
inscriptions—

*

One man looks at
another, whose head
tilts slightly downward, up, then down again,

as if looking away.

*

So what, that we're falling?

Until There's Nothing, Just the Sea,
a Sea of Leaves

We'd been up to the meadow. The wildflowers that had
seemed everywhere thinned gradually as we ascended, think
of an unbuttoned shirt falling soft in stages from a man's back,
shoulders first, now the strength of a good arm showing more
and more—and the chest, of course—the meadow cresting
until we came to where the horses had been buried, crosses
of thick vine—weathered, and ropelike—over two of them;
above the third, the presumed favorite, a cross of horseshoes
welded together, painted white. —Not out of boredom, but
because I've always found it difficult to resist looking down
from a great height, I looked away, down on the world that
we'd left behind us: how unimportant it seemed and, at the
same time, how very detailed. The skim and dart of blackbirds,
in their swiftness seeming to foil their own shadows—they
seemed to want to—and below that, the blighted orchard
whose trees could, in almost any light, make salvation look
like nothing so much as a script that, in the end, though
perhaps reluctantly, they'd been written out of . . . So much
for the world . . .

        It was then he turned to me as if turning were an art,
one he'd lost the mastery of, or as if some part of him, the part
more wounded, were caught inextricably in the kind of dream

in which one has been asked to say the difference between
mercy, compassion, and pity; and, to one's surprise, one
does know the difference, the answer comes as a star—clear,
attainable: blindly, a bit unsteadily—stutter of gratitude,
sway of despair—the hand rises, as if at last to reach for it.

Notes

The epigraph: Daniel Defoe, *Robinson Crusoe*, Random House, New York, 2001.

"Speak Low": The title is that of the Billie Holiday standard, written by Kurt Weill.

"Rubicon": The Rubicon is the river that Julius Caesar, returning from fighting in Gaul, crossed with his army into Italy, against orders from the Roman Senate, thereby precipitating civil war.

"Captivity": "Amazement grips me" is from Augustine's *Confessions* [X. viii (15)], as translated by Henry Chadwick, Oxford University Press, New York, 1991. In the same text, he divides human experience of time into memory, awareness, and expectation [XI. xx (26)].

"Distortion": See Augustine's *Confessions* [VIII. v (10)] for the relationship between the will, passion, habit, and hunger.

"Night Song": On suffering as a catalyst for patience, see the speech of Oedipus with which *Oedipus at Colonus* opens.

"Topaz": After being defeated in a flute-playing contest by Marsyas, Apollo flayed him alive.

"Late Empire": For the urns of happiness and woe, see Achilles' words to Priam in Homer's *Iliad*, Book XXIV.

"Naming the Stars": For Helen's question, see Homer's *Iliad*, Book III.

"The Plains of Troy": For Odysseus' response, see Sophocles, *Ajax*.

"A Little Moonlight": Lines 8–10 arise from the scene in which Apollo enters the Sibyl in Virgil's *Aeneid*, Book VI.

"Living Together": On force and its effects on the wielder of it and on its victim, see Simone Weil's essay "The *Iliad*, or the Poem of Force," as translated by Mary McCarthy in *War and the Iliad*, The New York Review of Books, New York, 2005.

ACKNOWLEDGMENTS

All thanks to the editors of the following publications, in which these poems—sometimes in different versions—originally appeared:

The American Scholar: "Cloud Country," "Directions from Here," "To Drown in Honey"

Asheville Poetry Review: "Lighting the Lamps"

Bliss: "Rubicon"

Boulevard: "Detachment," "The Moonflowers," "Now in Our Most Ordinary Voices," "Volition"

Cave Wall: "Happiness," "Reciprocity"

The Cincinnati Review: "Until There's Nothing, Just the Sea, a Sea of Leaves"

Columbia: "Landfall"

Columbia Poetry Review: "Husk"

CutBank: "Speak Low"

Field: "Captivity," "Gold on Parchment," "Porcelain," "Topaz"

Gulf Coast: "Night Song"

The Kenyon Review: "Conquest"

Knockout: "Fair Is Whatever the Gods Call Fair," "Mirror, Window, Mirror"

New England Review: "Distortion," "The River in Motion and in Stillness," "Storm"

The New York Times: "A Little Moonlight"

The New Yorker: "The Centaur"

Parnassus: Poetry in Review: "In a Perfect World," "Sterling"

Ploughshares: "Naming the Stars"

The Southern Quarterly: "Beautiful Dreamer"

TriQuarterly: "Southern Cross"

The Virginia Quarterly Review: "The Damned," "Late Empire"

Witness: "Living Together"

The Yale Review: "The Plains of Troy," "The Raft"

Printed in the USA
CPSIA information can be obtained
at www.ICGtesting.com
LVHW091148150724
785511LV00005B/624

9 780374 532161